# MAKING RUGS

by ANNE GILLESPIE LEWIS    pictures by G. OVERLIE

Lerner Publications Company • Minneapolis, Minnesota

LIBRARY OF CONGRESS CATALOGING IN PUBLICATION DATA

**Lewis, Anne Gillespie.**
  Making rugs.

  (An Early Craft Book)
  SUMMARY: Instructions for making hooked, braided, rya, felt, and other kinds of rugs and wall hangings from inexpensive materials such as discarded nylons, leftover yarn, and carpet remnants.

  1. Rugs—Juvenile literature.  [1. Rugs.  2. Handicraft]
  I. Overlie, George.  II. Title.

TT850.L45                    746.7                    76-13067
ISBN 0-8225-0876-1

*nal Standard Book Number: 0-8225-0876-1*
*Congress Catalog Card Number: 76-13067*

6  7  8  9  10  85  84  83  82  81  80  79  78  77  76

# Contents

# Rugs, then and now

Long ago, before houses had good heating systems, people kept out the cold and wind by making rugs and putting them on the floors and walls of their homes. The rugs kept the houses warmer, and they looked nice, too.

Today, though we have good heating, we still have rugs on the floors and sometimes on the walls. A wall rug is called a wall hanging. It is usually lighter in weight and less durable than a floor rug. Wall hangings are attractive. And floor rugs are both attractive and useful.

Small rugs by the front and back doors catch most of the dirt from shoes. Bath mats will prevent puddles of water from collecting when you step out of the bathtub or shower. Rugs placed on waxed floors will keep you from slipping. And soft, cozy rugs are comfortable to step on, especially when your feet are bare.

You will find it easy to make small rugs if you follow the directions in this book. These

5

rugs can also be used as wall hangings. When you have learned how to make the rugs described here, use your imagination to invent new designs and to make rugs from different materials. Let me know if you find out how to make a flying carpet!

There are many different types of rugs. Some of the best known rugs were made by the Persians. (Persia is now called Iran.) The Persians made rugs by knotting yarn into a backing, forming beautiful designs with the knots. Persian rugs are still being made.

Other kinds of Persian rugs are woven. There are no directions for a woven rug in this book, because you would need a loom to make one. Working with a rug loom is quite complicated.

Braided and hooked rugs are easy to make and inexpensive, too. American pioneer women often made them out of left-over materials or worn-out clothes.

Very simple rugs can be made by sewing

together pieces of material or by attaching one piece of material to another with tape or glue. You can also make a rug by cutting out a shape from a piece of heavy, fleecy material and decorating it.

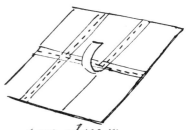

*tape edges on wrong side*

If you know someone who sews, knits, or crochets, that person may have leftover scraps of material or yarn you can use. Remember, you can substitute different materials for those given in the directions. If, for example, the directions call for rug yarn and you don't have rug yarn, use some other heavy yarn instead. Most department stores, yarn shops, and hobby shops have the materials and equipment you will need.

If you don't like the rug designs I describe, try making your own designs. Keep them simple, though, because detailed patterns in rugs are harder to make.

You can also make rugs that are larger or smaller than those described. But don't try to make a rug big enough to cover the whole floor

of a room. It would probably take you so long that you'd be grown-up before finishing it! Start with a rug you think you can make all by yourself. If you get tired before it is very big, use it for a pillow cover or wall hanging instead.

## A durable doormat

3 carpet samples

Because dirt and grit tracked in from the outdoors can ruin floors and carpets, a rug that catches outdoors dirt is useful. A durable doormat can be made from inexpensive carpet samples.

To make a doormat, get three carpet samples at a carpet store. I used samples 18 inches (45 centimeters) long and 9 inches (23 centimeters) wide. Your samples can be larger or smaller, but they should be of equal size. You will also need some very strong tape that is adhesive (sticky) on one side. Ordinary tape is not strong enough; carpet tape or any other strong tape is better.

carpet tape – or any other strong tape

Line the samples up, right sides down, as close to each other as possible without overlapping. Then cut a piece of tape the length of the samples. Fasten one sample piece to another with the tape. Press the tape down hard, half on one sample and half on the other. Tape the third sample to the other two. Put several more tape strips on the back of the doormat, so that they cross the first strips. These extra strips of tape will make the rug stronger.

This rug can be placed outside the front door or just inside the back door of your house or apartment. Before guests walk in, they can wipe their shoes on it.

## A felt rug

A felt rug is pretty and easy to make. It is not, however, as strong and durable as the other rugs in this book, so you will have to place it where it will not get much wear. It would be a nice rug to keep in a corner of your room. You might also want to hang it on a wall.

Because the rug is made of felt, it cannot be washed. It must be drycleaned. If you glue the finished rug to a larger piece of burlap or felt it will be much stronger.

To make a felt rug, you will need the following materials:

> six felt squares or rectangles of the same size in different colors
>
> felt scraps for designs
>
> a scissors
>
> white glue
>
> a pen or pencil
>
> newspaper for patterns
>
> a large piece of burlap or felt to back the finished rug. (This backing should be about two inches larger on all sides than the finished rug.)

Begin by gluing the felt pieces together. Put a line of glue about half an inch (about one centimeter) in from the edge of one piece. Press another piece down on the first, overlapping the edges and keeping them parallel. Let the glue

*glue ½" up from edge*

dry for about 20 minutes. Then put another line of glue on the opposite edge of the piece you just glued and press a third piece down on that. Make another row of squares the same way, allowing about 20 minutes after each step so the glue can dry. You will have two rows of three pieces each.

Join the two rows by putting a line of glue along the length of one row about an inch (two and one-half centimeters) from the edge. Carefully place the other row on the glued row, overlapping the edges and keeping them parallel. Press the second row down on the glued row and let the glue dry.

The basic shape of your felt rug is now defined. You can glue felt cutouts to each piece to make your rug more interesting. You might like cutouts in fruit shapes, such as an apple, an orange, bananas, grapes, a watermelon slice, or a pear. You might also like hand or footprints for designs. You could put one handprint and one footprint on each piece of the rug. Or you

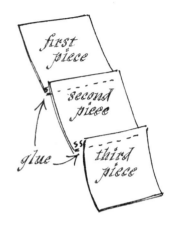

*glue another row the same as the first*

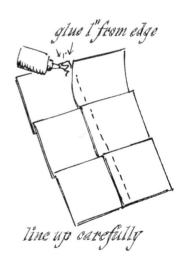

*line up carefully*

newspaper

make pattern ~ cut out ~
trace on contrasting
felt ~ carefully cut out

position on felt rug ~
then glue on felt design

burlap
backing

fringe

could cut out circles, triangles, squares, or other shapes.

To make sure that your designs are shaped as you'd like them to be, cut patterns for the shapes out of newspaper before you cut them out of the felt. Put the newspaper shapes on the rug. How do they look? Are they too big or too small? Should you move them to the left or right, or up or down? Do you like them just the way they are? When you have decided, cut out the final shapes from felt. Spread glue evenly over the back of each cutout and press it firmly onto the felt rug.

To make your rug stronger, cut out a piece of burlap or felt that is two inches wider and longer than your rug. Then spread glue evenly all over the back of the rug. Center it on the burlap or felt backing so that there are two inches of burlap or felt showing on every side. Press the rug down firmly and let the glue dry. To make an attractive fringe on the burlap backing, pull out the long threads on the border.

## An animal rug

Let's make an animal rug out of fake-fur fabric. I will tell you how to make a lion rug, but you can make another animal.

For a lion rug, you will need:

> a 24-inch-square (60-centimeter-square) piece of fur fabric in yellow or gold
>
> felt scraps in black, brown, and gold
>
> a scissors
>
> a pen or pencil
>
> newspaper for a pattern
>
> a ruler or tape measure
>
> white glue
>
> one and one-third yards (1.15 meters) of upholstery fringe at least two inches (five centimeters) wide
>
> a spool of black thread
>
> 16 yards (about 16 meters) of black or brown heavy yarn
>
> one-half yard (45 centimeters) of ribbon for a bow
>
> burlap cut to the exact size of the rug for a backing.

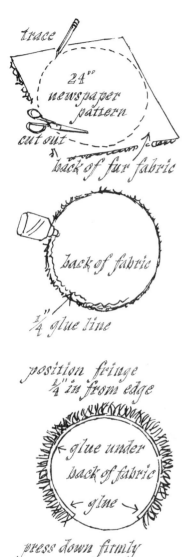

*trace*

*24" newspaper pattern*

*cut out*

*back of fur fabric*

*back of fabric*

*¼" glue line*

*position fringe ¼" in from edge*

*glue under back of fabric*

*glue*

*press down firmly*

Begin by making a circle pattern, 24 inches in diameter, out of newspaper. Then, using the pattern as a guide, draw the circle on the back of the fur fabric. Cut the circle out. If the material is very heavy, have a grown-up friend help you cut.

Now you are ready to make this circle look like a lion. One of the first things you'd notice about a lion, if you happened to run into one, would be its beautiful, thick mane. A lion also has a long tail ending in a tuft of hair. With the fringe and yarn, you will make a mane and tail for your lion rug. Make a face, too, with felt scraps.

Use the upholstery fringe for the mane. Put the fur fabric circle wrong-side up on the floor or a table and lay the fringe around the edge. It should reach about three-quarters of the way around the rug. Put a line of glue about one-quarter inch (one-half centimeter) in from the edge of the circle and lay the bound edge of the fringe on the glue line. Press the fringe down firmly onto the glue. When it dries, turn the lion right-side up and fluff out its fringe mane.

Then make a tail for your lion by braiding yarn. First cut the yarn into 24 pieces 24 inches (60 centimeters) long. Divide the yarn into three groups of eight pieces each and tie each group securely at the top with thread. Fasten the three bunches side by side onto a table or floor by taping them or by using a book to hold them down. Number the groups of yarn—"one" is the group on the left, "two" is in the middle, and "three" is on the right.

Now begin braiding by picking up "one" and putting it over "two." Next pick up "three" and put it over "one." Then put "two" over "three" and "one" over "two." Repeat the sequence again and again. It is easier to do it than to read about it.

As you braid, pull slightly on each bunch of yarn so that the braid will be firm. When you have about three or four inches (eight or ten centimeters) of yarn yet unbraided, quit and

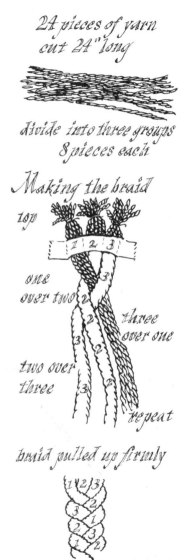

24 pieces of yarn cut 24" long

divide into three groups 8 pieces each

Making the braid

top

one over two

three over one

two over three

repeat

braid pulled up firmly

ribbon

thread is
under ribbon

back
of rug

glue

finished lion rug!

Lion rug with legs
and head

fasten all the strands of yarn together by winding thread around them several times and knotting it. Put a ribbon bow over the thread. Glue the upper end of the braid to the underside of the rug in the middle of the space where there is no mane.

Then cut out circles of black or green felt for the eyes, a black triangle for a nose, and black half circles for the ears. Glue them onto the rug opposite the tail. Press the felt down firmly so that it will hold fast to the fur. Now spread out your burlap backing and dot it with white glue. Carefully lay the lion rug on its backing and press down firmly. Your lion rug is finished!

A round animal rug, like the lion, is the simplest to make. But you can also make an animal with legs and a head. If you do, make a pattern that includes the legs and head so that the main part of your rug is cut from one piece of fabric.

## Traditional rugs

The next three rugs are more difficult than the rugs you have learned to make so far. But they are well worth the effort, for they are both durable and attractive. These three rugs are traditional—that is, people have been making them for many years. American pioneer women made braided and hooked rugs. And there are countless variations of pile rugs.

*Braided*

*Hooked*

*Pile*

## A braided rug

A braided rug is the easiest of the three rugs to make. Pioneer women made rugs of their worn-out clothes by cutting them into strips and braiding them. It was almost like getting something for nothing. You, too, can make a braided rug for almost nothing.

Instead of using old clothes, which take some time to prepare for braiding, you can use worn-out nylon stockings and panty hose. Ask friends and relatives if they will save their torn pairs

wash and dry your
rug material

cut off feet and top

use each leg as 1 strand

for you. You may also have colored tights that are outgrown or worn-out. To braid a rug, you will need 60 stocking legs, or thirty pairs of panty hose and tights.

First, wash and dry all the pantyhose and stockings. Then cut off the feet and the panty part. All sixty of the legs should be the same length. (About 10 inches, or 25 centimeters, is a good length.)

Now begin braiding. Use each leg as a strand. With brown thread, tie three strands together about an inch from one end. Braid the strands as you did the lion's tail. When you come to within an inch of the end of the strands, tie the braid again with brown thread.

After you have made twenty braids, you can lace them together to make a small rectangular rug. (Work at a table or desk to do so.) You will need a large needle with a blunt point and a spool of brown carpet thread. Thread the needle and make a knot in one end of the thread. To make a knot, wrap the strand of thread around your index finger several times. Then roll the thread back and forth between your thumb and index finger. The thread will begin to form a knot with the rolling. As you pull the thread away from your index finger, pinch the ball of thread between the index finger and thumb, and pull it tight. It will form a firm knot.

To begin lacing the braids together, push the needle through the first braid at one end. Pull the thread until the knot is firm against the braid. Wrap the thread several times around the braid once again.

Now put another braid alongside the first one. Work the needle back and forth between the two braids. Do not sew through the material, but pass the needle through the spaces between the strands of the braids. Lace just the strands that lie against each other together. When you have worked your way to the opposite ends of the braids, wind the thread around those ends a few times. Then lace a third braid to the second braid, working upward this time. Pro-

make 20 of these

lacing 2 braids together

ceed in this way until you have laced all the braids together. As you work, be sure to pull the thread gently so that the lacing will not produce gaps between the braids. The thread should be almost invisible.

Round and oval braided rugs, though more common than the straight braided rug, are more difficult to put together. And they take more time and stockings. (You might need several hundred pair.) But round or oval rugs are very attractive.

If you would like to try one of these rugs, here are the basic steps: first sew several stocking or pantyhose legs together end to end. When you sew the end of one leg to another, you should sew them at right angles to each other. (If you were making a braided rug out of strips of cloth, you would do the same thing.) To make a right angle, put the two legs together to make the letter "L." With small running (in and out) stitches, sew a diagonal seam where the legs overlap. Then cut off the overlapped triangular

*Round or oval braided rugs*

*to sew two pantyhose legs together*

*stitch*

*trim off ¼" from stitching*

corners about one-fourth inch (one-half centimeter) away from your stitching and unfold the legs. You will see that the stocking legs form a straight strand.

When you have a strand about three feet (one meter) long, make two more strands just like the first. Now you can begin to braid. Fasten the three strands together by winding and tying thread around the tops.

You should work at a table to keep your rug flat. Put a heavy book or board on the top of the strands so you won't have to hold them down as you braid. Thread a blunt-ended needle with carpet thread and have it ready. Keep several large safety pins at hand, too.

You will not be braiding a straight braid but a braid that curves in a circular shape. Therefore, every time you want to round a corner, pull harder on the inner strand of the braid. Start lacing the braids together as soon as your braid begins to take shape. But first pin the rug with safety pins to guide you as you lace. Then

*tie with thread*

*three strands each 3' long*

*work on a flat surface*

*pin together as you braid*

*pull harder on the inner strand*

*lace together from underside of the rug ~ do not lace too tightly*

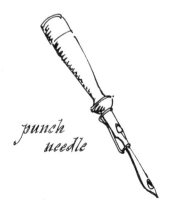

*punch needle*

lace from the underside of the rug, making sure the tied ends of the first strands show only on the bottom of the rug. Add stocking lengths as you run out of strands to braid. As the rug gets larger, you will not have to pull as hard on the inner corner of the braid when you want to round a corner. And do not lace the braid too tightly. A tight braid will make a hump in the rug. When the rug is as large as you want it, finish it by stitching the ends of the braid onto the underside of the rug.

The rug can last for many years. When it gets dirty, just throw it in the washing machine and hang it up to dry. And if you want your room to have an Early American look, this rug will fit perfectly.

## A hooked rug

Hooked rugs are fluffy and nice to step on. They are also quite easy to make once you learn how to use the special punch needle that does the job.

Though we will use a punch needle to make a hooked rug, there are other ways to make them. Years ago rug-makers used crochet hooks to hook rugs from bits and pieces of material or yarn.

These are the things you will need to make a small hooked rug:

> one punch needle (You can get one in a yarn store, and it won't cost very much.)
>
> a 24-inch-square (60-centimeter-square) piece of closely woven burlap
>
> four four-ounce (112-gram) skeins of thick wool or acrylic yarn in different colors
>
> one two-ounce (56-gram) skein of thick wool or acrylic yarn in another color
>
> rubberized latex
>
> a pen or pencil
>
> a yardstick or meter stick
>
> iron-on seam binding.

Using a ruler, draw a two-inch (five-centi-

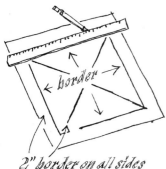

2" border on all sides
draw diagonal lines
to corners
wind yarn into a ball

Threading the punch

through
hole →

meter) border on all four sides of the burlap. Next, draw an "X" on the burlap by connecting the diagonal corners with intersecting lines. When you are finished with the rug, it will have four triangles of different colors. And each will be bordered on its two equal sides by a fifth color.

You will use the punch needle on the wrong side of the rug. The side with the border and the "X" drawn on it is the wrong side. You will be punching in lines running parallel to the lines you have drawn.

Before you start the rug, try the punch on a spare piece of burlap to acquaint yourself with the technique. Wind the yarn from one of the skeins into a ball. Then thread the punch with the end of the yarn. To thread the punch, push the yarn into the hole nearest the handle, slide it through the groove and out through the hole near the point.

Hold the threaded punch in your "best" hand as you would hold a pencil. Push the punch through the weave of the burlap until it is stopped by the wire guide. With your other hand, reach under the burlap and grasp the yarn at the tip of the punch. Now slowly pull the punch toward you, keeping hold of the yarn with your other hand. When the tip of the punch has barely come back through on the wrong side of the burlap, move it a thread or two away from the first punch and push it through again, letting go of the first loop. As the second punch comes through, grasp the yarn on the tip of the punch again. While you work, keep the punch close to the burlap and keep the point of the punch facing in the same direction. You will make the whole rug this way.

When you have practiced enough to feel at ease with the punch, you can start to hook the rug. Hook the "X" part of the rug first, because it will take less time and will serve as a guide for the rest of the rug. You should punch three rows of loops on both sides of the "X" lines. If the middle of the "X" gets too bulky as you

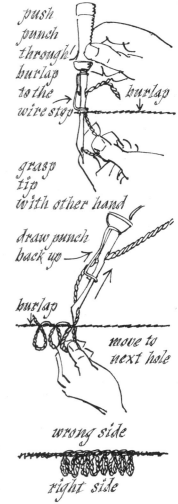

push punch through! burlap to the wire stop

burlap

grasp tip with other hand

draw punch back up →

burlap

move to next hole

wrong side

right side

*punch 3 rows of loops on each side of "X"*

*then finish each triangle start from bottom corner*

*bottom side*

*hook 2 or 3 rows ~ then cut the loops carefully*

hook, punch only six rows of loops through it. Cut the yarn on the intersecting line and skip across the six rows to pick up the design again.

Keep the rows close enough together so that you cannot see burlap between the loops. To make sure no burlap shows, turn the rug over now and then to check the right side of the rug. If you can see burlap, make the rows and the punches closer together.

After you have finished the "X," begin hooking the triangles. It is easiest to start from a bottom corner. Hook the first rows nearest the sides of the triangle and then hook several rows across the bottom. Fill in the center by hooking rows parallel to the first rows you made.

Be sure to keep the punch tool close to the fabric. If you do not, and pull too hard on the punch, an entire row might rip out. For this reason, you may want to cut the loops on the right side of the rug as you go along. Hook two or three rows and cut the loops at the top.

But if you'd like to leave the loops uncut, you should cover the back of the rug with rubberized latex when it is finished. (You can get this at a craft or hobby shop.) Follow the directions on the can for applying the latex.

for rugs with uncut loops

The last step in making a hooked rug of this type is hemming it. You can sew a hem with a needle and heavy thread, which is rather hard work. You can also hem the rug with iron-on seam binding. This is easier and quite durable. First cut the corners from the burlap border near the corner of the loops. This will eliminate bulky material in the hem. Now turn the rug over and fold the burlap border back. Fasten it down by pressing iron-on binding over the fold.

cut off burlap corner
~ turn rug over ~ fold
burlap border back

iron-on
binding

placed over fold

If you have used wool yarn, this rug should not be washed. Take it to the drycleaner if it gets dirty. This is a nice rug to step on when you get out of bed on cold mornings.

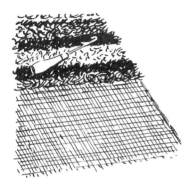

# A pile rug

A pile rug is similar to a hooked rug. It is made by tying knots of yarn onto a backing with either a needle or another tool called a latch hook. This rug is called a pile, or rya (RYE-ah), rug and can be looped or cut. A pile rug is very sturdy, lush, and beautiful.

You will need the following things to make a small pile rug:

an 18-by-20-inch (45-by-50-centimeter) piece of double mesh canvas with approximately four holes to the inch for a backing. (You can buy this in a yarn shop.)

several large, blunt needles with eyes big enough to hold several strands of yarn, or a latch hook

18 ounces (504 grams) of rug yarn in different colors for the needle method; 14 one-ounce (28-gram) packages of pre-cut yarn for the latch hook method.

Begin by drawing a one-inch (two-and-one-half-centimeter) border on all four sides of the canvas.

Let's learn how to tie rug knots with a needle first. Thread the needle with three strands of yarn, each about 18 inches long. Starting on the top side of the backing, push the needle from the top into the first hole at the corner of the bottom and left border lines. Then push the needle under the double mesh threads next to that hole and up into the next hole. Pull the needle through until two inches (five centimeters) of yarn are left protruding from the first hole. Hold these ends down with the thumb of your other hand to keep them from pulling through. Bring the needle back to the two double mesh strands to the left of the first hole. (Keep the two-inch strand held down to keep the pathway clear.) Push the needle down under these threads and up into the first hole, pulling the yarn until it makes a knot. Take your thumb from the yarn ends.

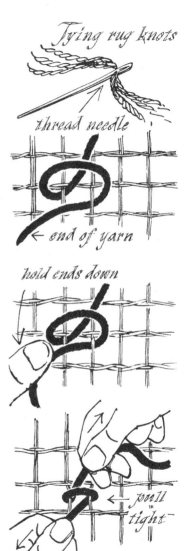

*Tying rug knots*

*thread needle*

*← end of yarn*

*hold ends down*

*← pull tight*

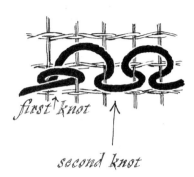

first knot

second knot

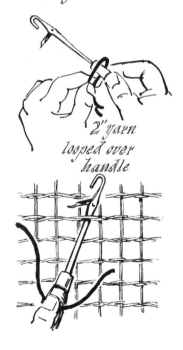

Using the latch hook

2" yarn looped over handle

Make another knot one space away from the second hole. This time you will leave a two-inch yarn *loop* protruding from the first hole. Finish the knot as you did the first time. When you come to the end of a yarn length or a row, push the needle over the mesh threads and down through the second hole to the back. Cut the thread. You can cut the loops open or leave them uncut, as you wish.

To tie knots with a latch hook, use the pre-cut yarn. The strands will be about two inches long.

First, loop a strand of pre-cut yarn over the wooden handle of the latch hook tool with your left hand. (If you are left-handed, use your right hand with this step, and use the opposite hand from the one mentioned in each of the following steps.) Then, at a corner, push the top of the hook (with the latch open) down through the first hole, under the threads, and up through the second hole. Push the hook up far enough so that the latch clears the threads of the canvas.

With your left hand still on the yarn, pull the ends of it up to the mesh and over the open latch in the second hole. Hold the yarn ends in place. With your other hand, pull the hook toward you. The latch will close, holding the yarn between it and the hook. The hook will carry the ends of yarn through the loop in the first hole, forming a knot. Repeat this process in each adjoining space, working across the narrow side of the mesh backing. You'll see how simple this is once you've done a knot or two.

You can use either the needle method or the latch hook method to make a pile rug, or you can use both for a difference in pile lengths. You can use different colors and make strips several rows wide, or you can make every row a different color. You can make splotches of color, since each knot is tied individually. You can draw a design on the mesh and fill it in with knots of a contrasting color. To finish your rug, hem it as you did the hooked rug.

When you have completed a rug of any kind,

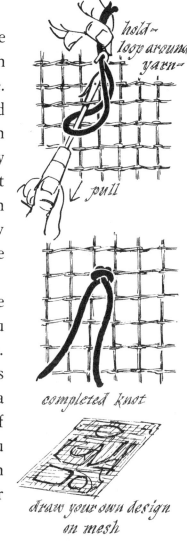

hold~
loop around
yarn~

↙ pull

completed knot

draw your own design
on mesh

print your name and the date you finished it on the back. I know you will feel proud when you have finished a rug. It will be attractive, useful, long-lasting, and will give you a real feeling of accomplishment.